D0840962

To:

_____

From:

_____

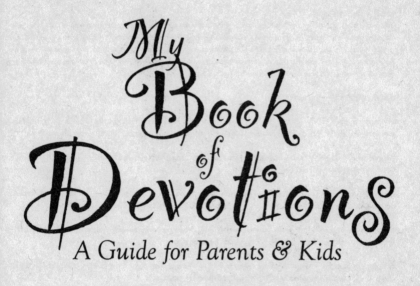

My Book of Devotions

A Guide for Parents & Kids

about Patience

Simon & Schuster, Inc.

NEW YORK LONDON TORONTO SYDNEY

Simon & Schuster, Inc.
1230 Avenue of the Americas, New York, New York 10020

© 2005 Freeman-Smith, LLC.

The quoted ideas expressed in this book (but not Scripture verses) are not, in all cases, exact quotations, as some have been edited for clarity and brevity. In all cases, the author has attempted to maintain the speaker's original intent. In some cases, quoted material for this book was obtained from secondary sources, primarily print media. While every effort was made to ensure the accuracy of these sources, the accuracy cannot be guaranteed. For additions, deletions, corrections, or clarifications in future editions of this text, please write Freeman-Smith, LLC.

Scripture quotations are taken from:

Scriptures marked NIV® are from the *Holy Bible, New International Version®*. Copyright © 1973, 1978, 1984 by International Bible Society. Used by permission of Zondervan Publishing House. All rights reserved.

Scriptures marked NKJV are taken from the *New King James Version®*. Copyright © 1982 by Thomas Nelson, Inc. Used by permission. All rights reserved.

Scriptures marked NLT are taken from the *Holy Bible, New Living Translation*. Copyright © 1996. Used by permission of Tyndale House Publishers, Inc., Wheaton, Illinois 60189. All rights reserved.

Scriptures marked NCV are quoted from *The Holy Bible, New Century Version*. Copyright © 1987, 1988, 1991 by Word Publishing, Nashville, TN 37214. Used by permission.

Scripture quotations marked MSG are taken from *The Message*. Copyright © by Eugene H. Peterson 1993, 1994, 1995. Used by permission of NavPress Publishing Group.

Scripture quotations marked ICB are taken from the *International Children's Bible, New Century Version*. Copyright © 1986, 1988 by Word Publishing, Nashville, TN 37214. Used by permission.

Scripture quotations marked Holman CSB are taken from the *Holman Christian Standard Bible®*. Copyright © 1999, 2000, 2002, 2003 by Holman Bible Publishers. Used by permission. Holman Christian Standard Bible®, Holman CSB®, and HCSB® are federally registered trademarks of Holman Bible Publishers.

Cover Design by Kim Russell / Wahoo Designs
Page Layout by Bart Dawson

Manufactured in the United States of America

10 9 8 7 6 5 4 3 2 1

ISBN-13: 978-1-4169-1598-0
ISBN-10: 1-4169-1598-2

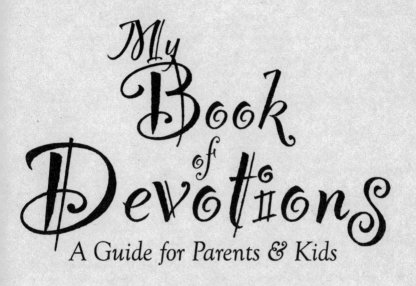

My Book of Devotions

A Guide for Parents & Kids

about Patience

Love is patient; love is kind.

1 Corinthians 13:4 HCSB

Table of Contents

A Message for Parents

The fact that you've picked up this book means that you're a concerned, thoughtful parent—congratulations. When you spend time reading to your youngster, you're helping your child build a strong intellectual and spiritual foundation.

This little book—which is intended to be read by Christian parents to their young children—contains 31 brief chapters, one for each day of the month. Each chapter consists of a Bible verse, a brief story or lesson, kid-friendly quotations from notable Christian thinkers, a tip, and a prayer. Every chapter examines a different aspect of an important Biblical theme: patience.

For the next 31 days, take the time to read one chapter each night to your child, and then spend a few moments talking about the chapter's meaning. By the end of the month, you will have had 31 different opportunities to share God's wisdom with your son or daughter, and that's good.

If you have been touched by God's love and His grace, then you know the joy that He has brought into your own life. Now it's your turn to share His message with the boy or girl whom He has entrusted to your care. Happy reading! And may God richly bless you and your family now and forever.

Patience Is . . .

Always be humble and gentle.
Be patient and accept each other with love.
Ephesians 4:2 ICB

Day 1

The dictionary defines the word "patience" as "the ability to be calm, tolerant, and understanding." Here's what that means: the word "calm" means being in control of your emotions (not letting your emotions control you). The word "tolerant" means being kind and considerate to people who are different from you. And, the word "understanding" means being able to put yourself in another person's shoes.

If you can be calm, tolerant, and understanding, you will be the kind of person whose good deeds are a blessing to your family and friends. They will appreciate your good deeds, and so will God.

Big Idea for Kids

Since you want other people to be patient with you, you should be patient with them, too.

Be patient. God is using today's difficulties to strengthen you for tomorrow.

Max Lucado

Big Idea for Parents

Patience starts with you! Kids imitate their parents, so act accordingly! The best way for your child to learn to be patient is by example . . . your example!

Today's Prayer

Dear Lord, sometimes it's hard to be a patient person, and that's exactly when I should try my hardest to be patient. Help me to follow Your commandments by being a patient, loving Christian, even when it's hard.

Amen

It's Better To Be Patient

Moderation is better than muscle,
self-control better than political power.
Proverbs 16:32 MSG

Day 2

In the Book of Proverbs, we are told that patience is a very good thing. But for most of us, patience can also be a very hard thing. After all, we have many things that we want, and we want them NOW! But the Bible tells us that we must learn to wait patiently for the things that God has in store for us.

Are you having trouble being patient? If so, remember that patience takes practice, and lots of it, so keep trying. And if you make a mistake, don't be too upset. After all, if you're going to be a really patient person, you shouldn't just be patient with others; you should also be patient with yourself.

Big Idea for Kids

Take a deep breath, a very deep breath: if you think you're about to say or do something you'll regret later, slow down and take a deep breath, or two deep breaths, or ten, or . . . well, you get the point.

> God is never in a hurry.
> Oswald Chambers

Big Idea for Parents

Talk it over: if your child has done something that is impulsive, discourteous, or dangerous, your natural response will be anger. But as soon as you calm down, help your child learn from the experience by talking about the behavior, its motivations, and its consequences.

Today's Prayer

Dear Lord, the Bible tells me
that it's better to be patient
than impulsive. Help me to slow myself
down so I can make better decisions
today and every day.
Amen

Waiting for Your Turn

Let everyone see that you are
considerate in all you do.
Philippians 4:5 NLT

Day 3

When we're standing in line or waiting for our turn, it's tempting to scream, "Me first!" It's tempting, but it's the wrong thing to do! The Bible tells us that we shouldn't push ahead of other people; instead, we should do the right thing—and the polite thing—by saying, "You first!"

Sometimes, waiting your turn can be hard, especially if you're excited or in a hurry. But even then, waiting patiently is the right thing to do. Why? Because parents say so, teachers say so, and, most importantly, God says so!

Big Idea for Kids

The next time you're standing in line, don't try to push ahead of your neighbors. After all, if you don't want other people breaking in front of you, then you shouldn't break in front of them!

What is your focus today?
Joy comes when it is Jesus first,
others second...then you.

Kay Arthur

Big Idea for Parents

When it comes to courteous behavior, you're the most important role model: so pay careful attention to the way that you treat other people, especially those who are not in a position to help you. For further instructions, read Matthew 25:40.

Today's Prayer

Dear Lord, let me be a courteous
person. Let me treat other people
with patience and respect.
And, let the things that I say and do
show my family and friends that
I love them . . . and You.
Amen

Speaking the Right Words at the Right Time

A word spoken at the right time is like golden apples on a silver tray.

Proverbs 25:11 HCSB

Day 4

Sometimes, it's easier to say the wrong thing than it is to say the right thing—especially if we're in a hurry to blurt out the first words that come into our heads. But, if we are patient and if we choose our words carefully, we can help other people feel better, and that's exactly what God wants us to do.

The Book of Proverbs tells us that the right words, spoken at the right time, can be wonderful gifts to our families and to our friends. That's why we should think about the things that we say before we say them, not after. When we do, our words make the world a better place, and that's exactly what God wants!

Big Idea for Kids

To find golden words, use the Golden Rule: when choosing the right words to say to someone else, think about the words that you would want to hear if you were standing in their shoes.

Attitude and the spirit in which we
communicate are as important
as the words we say.
Charles Stanley

Big Idea for Parents

There are so many ways to say, "I love you." Find them. Put love notes in lunch pails and on pillows; hug relentlessly; laugh, play, and pray with abandon. Remember that love is highly contagious, and that your task, as a parent, is to ensure that your children catch it.

Today's Prayer

Dear Lord, if I choose my words
carefully, I can make everybody
happier, including myself. Today and
every day, help me choose the words
that You want me to speak so that
I can make my corner of the world
a better place to live.
Amen

Praying for Patience

Do not worry about anything,
but pray and ask God for everything
you need, always giving thanks.
Philippians 4:6 NCV

Would you like to become a more patient person? Pray about it. Is there a person you don't like? Pray for a forgiving heart. Do you lose your temper more than you should? Ask God for help.

Whatever you need, ask God to help you. And, as you pray more, you'll discover that God is always near and that He's always ready to hear from you. So don't worry about things; pray about them. God is waiting . . . and listening!

Big Idea for Kids

Pray early and often: One way to make sure that your heart is in tune with God is to pray often. The more you talk to God, the more He will talk to you.

Prayer is not a weakness but a strength. Its benefits are patience, insight, endurance, and the power to cope with anything.

Franklin Graham

Big Idea for Parents

Make yours a house of prayer: Prayer changes things, and it changes families. Make certain that it changes yours.

Today's Prayer

Dear Lord, You are always near;
let me talk with You often.
When I am impatient, let me turn
to You. And, let me use prayer to find
the peace that You desire for my life
today and every day.
Amen

When You're Angry

Patient people have great understanding,
but people with quick tempers
show their foolishness.
Proverbs 14:29 NCV

When you're angry, you will be tempted to say things and do things that you'll regret later. But don't do them! Instead of doing things in a hurry, slow down long enough to calm yourself down.

Jesus does not intend that you strike out against other people, and He doesn't intend that your heart be troubled by anger. Your heart should instead be filled with love, just like Jesus' heart was . . . and is!

Big Idea for Kids

Time out! If you become angry, the time to step away from the situation is before you say unkind words or do unkind things—not after. It's perfectly okay to place yourself in "time out" until you can calm down.

> When you strike out in anger,
> you may miss the other person,
> but you will always hit yourself.
> Jim Gallery

Big Idea for Parents

Getting enough sleep? If you find yourself short on patience, perhaps you're also short on sleep. If so, turn off the TV and go to bed. As your energy returns, so will your patience.

Today's Prayer

Dear Lord, help me not to be
an angry person, but instead, make me
a forgiving person. Fill my heart not
with anger, but with love for
others . . . and for You.
Amen

How Patient Would Jesus Be?

Let me give you a new command:
Love one another. In the same way
I loved you, you love one another.
John 13:34 MSG

Day 7

If you've lost patience with someone, or if you're angry, take a deep breath and then ask yourself a simple question: "How would Jesus behave if He were here?" The answer to that question will tell you what to do.

Jesus was quick to speak kind words, and He was quick to forgive others. We must do our best to be like Him. When we do, we will be patient, loving, understanding, and kind.

Big Idea for Kids

When in doubt: do the thing that you think Jesus would do. And, of course, don't do something if you think that He wouldn't do it.

In the name of Jesus Christ who was never in a hurry, we pray, O God, that You will slow us down, for we know that we live too fast.

Peter Marshall

Big Idea for Parents

It starts with parents: Our children will learn about Jesus at church and, in some cases, at school. But, the ultimate responsibility for religious teachings should never be delegated to institutions outside the home. As parents, we must teach our children about the love and grace of Jesus Christ by our words and by our actions.

Today's Prayer

Dear Lord, let me use Jesus as
my example for living. When I have
questions about what to do or how
to act, let me behave as He behaved.
When I do so, I will be patient,
loving, and kind, not just today,
but every day.
Amen

If at First You Don't Succeed

But the people who trust in the Lord will become strong again. They will rise up as an eagle in the sky. They will run without needing rest. They will walk without becoming tired.

Isaiah 40:31 ICB

Day 8

Perhaps you've tried to become a more patient person, but you're still falling back into your old habits. If so, don't be discouraged. Instead, be even more determined to become the person God wants you to be.

If you trust God, and if you keep asking Him to help you change bad habits, He will help you make yourself into a new person. So, if at first you don't succeed, keep praying. God is listening, and He's ready to help you become a better person if you ask Him . . . so ask Him!

Big Idea for Kids

Forgive . . . and then forgive some more! Sometimes, you may forgive someone once and then, at a later time, you may become angry at that very same person again. If so, you must forgive that person again . . . and again . . . until it sticks!

We are all on our way somewhere.
We'll get there if we just keep going.
Barbara Johnson

Big Idea for Parents

Wait patiently for your child to grow up. Some bad habits, like impulsive behaviors and temper tantrums, are simply a sign of youthful immaturity. If you maintain a steady hand, a loving heart, and a level head, the bad behavior will, in all likelihood, subside as your child matures.

Today's Prayer

Dear Lord, help me to become a person whose habits are pleasing to You. Help me to change my bad habits so that nothing can interfere with my love for others or with my love for You.

Amen

The Golden Rule and Patience

Do for other people the same things
you want them to do for you.
Matthew 7:12 ICB

Day 9

Jesus gave us a Golden Rule for living: He said that we should treat other people in the same way that we want to be treated. And because we want other people to be patient with us, we, in turn, must be patient with them.

Being patient with other people means treating them with kindness, respect, and understanding. It means waiting our turn when we're standing in line and forgiving our friends when they've done something we don't like. Sometimes, it's hard to be patient, but we've got to do our best. And when we do, we're following the Golden Rule—God's rule for how to treat others—and everybody wins!

Big Idea for Kids

What's good for you is good for them, too: If you want others to be patient with you, then you should treat them in the same way. That's the Golden Rule, and it should be your rule, too!

> Seek to do good, and you will find that happiness will run after you.
> James Freeman Clarke

Big Idea for Parents

"The least of these . . . .": How did Jesus treat the people who lived on the edges of society? With patience, respect, and love. Hopefully, all of our children will see that same behavior reflected in the actions of their parents.

Today's Prayer

Dear Lord, make me a patient person
and let me be a person who
observes the Golden Rule.
Let me be understanding and kind,
and let me be quick to forgive others,
just as You have forgiven me.
Amen

There's a Time for Everything

There is a time for everything,
and a season for every activity under heaven.
Ecclesiastes 3:1 NIV

Day 10

We human beings can be so impatient. We know what we want, and we know exactly when we want it: RIGHT NOW! But, God knows better. He has created a world that unfolds according to His own timetable, not ours.

As Christians, we must be patient as we wait for God to show us the wonderful plans that He has in store for us. And while we're waiting for God to make His plans clear, let's keep praying and keep giving thanks to the One who has given us more blessings than we can count.

Big Idea for Kids

Big, bigger, and very big plans. God has very big plans in store for your life, so trust Him and wait patiently for those plans to unfold. And remember: God's timing is best.

Your times are in His hands.
He's in charge of the timetable,
so wait patiently.

Kay Arthur

Big Idea for Parents

Sometimes, the answer to prayer is "No." God doesn't grant all of our requests, nor should He. We must help our children understand that our prayers are answered by a sovereign, all-knowing God, and that we must trust His answers.

Today's Prayer

Dear Lord, sometimes I become
impatient for things to happen.
Sometimes, I want the world to unfold
according to my plan, not Yours.
Help me to remember, Lord, that
Your plan is best for me, not just for
today, but for all eternity.
Amen

Being Patient with Brothers, Sisters, and Cousins

Show respect for all people.
Love the brothers and sisters
of God's family.
1 Peter 2:17 ICB

Day 11

How easy is it to become angry with our brothers, sisters, and cousins? Sometimes, very easy! It's silly, but it's true: sometimes we can become angry with the very people we love the most.

The Bible tells us to be patient with everybody, and that most certainly includes brothers and sisters (if we're lucky enough to have them). We must also be patient and kind to our cousins and friends. Why? Because it's the right thing to do, and because it's God's commandment. Enough said!

Big Idea for Kids

Say it! If you love your brother or sister (and, of course, you do!) say so. But don't stop there: let all your family members know that you love them . . . a lot!

> The family that prays together,
> stays together.
>
> Anonymous

Big Idea for Parents

Parents set the tone: As parents, it's up to us to establish the general tone and content of the conversations that take place in our homes. Let's make certain that the words we speak are worthy of the One we worship.

Today's Prayer

Dear Lord, let me be respectful
of all people, starting with my family
and friends. And, let me share
the love that I feel in my heart
with them . . . and with You!
Amen

Angry Feelings Get in the Way

My dear brothers, always be willing
to listen and slow to speak. Do not become
angry easily. Anger will not help you
live a good life as God wants.

James 1:19 ICB

Day 12

In the Book of James, we learn that God has a "good life" that He wants each of us to live. But if we lose patience and become angry with others, our own anger can interfere with God's plans.

Do you want the good life that God has planned for you? If so, don't let your own anger get in the way. In other words, don't interfere with your own happiness. Instead, calm down and get ready for the wonderful life that God has promised to those whose hearts are filled with patience and with love.

Big Idea for Kids

Think carefully . . . make that very carefully! If you're a little angry, think carefully before you speak. If you're very angry, think very carefully. Otherwise, you might say something in anger that you would regret later.

> Revenge is the raging fire that consumes the arsonist.
>
> Max Lucado

Big Idea for Parents

Don't fan the flames: When your children become angry or upset, you'll tend to become angry and upset, too. Resist that temptation. As the grown-up person in the family, it's up to you to remain calm, even when other, less mature members of the family, can't.

Today's Prayer

Dear Lord, when I am not patient, remind me that it's better to stop and think things through than it is to rush ahead without thinking. Make me a patient person, Lord, and fill me with consideration for others and love for You.

Amen

Listening to God

The thing you should want most is
God's kingdom and doing what God wants.
Then all these other things you
need will be given to you.
Matthew 6:33 ICB

God has a perfect idea of the kind of people He wants us to become. And for starters, He wants us to be loving, kind, and patient—not rude or mean!

The Bible tells us that God is love and that if we wish to know Him, we must have love in our hearts. Sometimes, of course, when we're tired, angry, or frustrated, it is very hard for us to be loving. Thankfully, anger and frustration are feelings that come and go, but God's love lasts forever.

If you'd like to become a more patient person, talk to God in prayer, listen to what He says, and share His love with your family and friends. God is always listening, and He's ready to talk to you . . . now!

Big Idea for Kids

Quiet please! This world is LOUD! To hear what God has to say, you'll need to turn down the music and turn off the television long enough for God to get His message through.

In prayer, the ear is of first importance.
It is of equal importance with the tongue,
but the ear must be named first.
We must listen to God.
S. D. Gordon

Big Idea for Parents

If silence is golden, reading is silver: how precious are the hours we spend reading to our children and with them. In those quiet moments, they are blessed, and so, of course, are we.

Today's Prayer

Dear Lord, help me remember
the importance of prayer.
You always hear my prayers, God;
let me always pray them!
Amen

Being a Patient Friend

A friend loves you all the time,
and a brother helps in time of trouble.
Proverbs 17:17 NCV

Day 14

Having friends requires patience. From time to time, even our most considerate friends may do things that make us angry. Why? Because they are not perfect. Neither, of course, are we.

Today and every day, let us be understanding and patient with our friends. If we forgive them when they make mistakes, then perhaps they will forgive us when we make mistakes. And then, because we are patient and forgiving with each other, we will build friendships that will last.

Big Idea for Kids

If you're having trouble forgiving someone else . . . think how many times other people have forgiven you!

Just thinking about a friend makes you
want to do a happy dance, because
a friend is someone who loves you
in spite of your faults.
Charles Schulz

Big Idea for Parents

Encouragement 101: Take every opportunity to teach your children ways to encourage other people. And, while you're at it, make your own home an oasis of encouragement in a difficult world.

Today's Prayer

Dear Lord, let me be patient and understanding toward my friends. Lord, help me to remember that we all make mistakes and to forgive them, like You have forgiven me.

Amen

It's Up to You

We must not become tired of doing good.
We will receive our harvest of eternal life
at the right time. We must not give up!
Galatians 6:9 ICB

Day 15

Nobody can be patient for you. You've got to be patient for yourself. Certainly your parents can teach you about patience, but when it comes to controlling your temper, nobody can control it for you; you've got to control it yourself.

In the Book of Galatians, Paul writes, "We must not tire of doing good." And that's an important lesson: even when we're tired or frustrated, we must do our best to do the right thing.

So the next time you're tempted to lose your temper, stop for a moment and remember that when it comes to good deeds and good behavior, it's up to you.

Big Idea for Kids

Don't try to blame other people for the mistakes you make . . . When you point your finger at someone else, the rest of your fingers are pointing back at you!

Simply stated, self-discipline is obedience
to God's Word and willingness to submit
everything in life to His will,
for His ultimate glory.

John MacArthur

Big Idea for Parents

Excuses, excuses, excuses: As parents of young children, we hear lots and lots of excuses, some of which are valid, but many of which are not. It's our job to determine the difference between valid excuses and imaginary ones, and then to help our children understand the difference between the two.

Today's Prayer

Dear Lord, there is a right way
and a wrong way to behave.
Let me remember that it's my job
to behave myself and to be the kind
of Christian that I know You want me
to be . . . today and always.

Amen

Stop and Think

Wise people's minds tell them what to say,
and that helps them be better teachers.
Proverbs 16:23 NCV

Day 16

When we lose control of our emotions, we do things that we shouldn't do. Sometimes, we throw tantrums. How silly! Other times we pout or whine. Too bad!

The Bible tells us that it is foolish to become angry and that it is wise to remain calm. That's why we should learn to slow down and to think about things before we do them.

Do you want to make life better for yourself and for your family? Then be patient and think things through. Stop and think before you do things, not after. It's the wise thing to do.

Big Idea for Kids

Tantrums? No way! If you think you might lose your temper, stop and catch your breath, and walk away if you must. It's better to walk away than it is to let your temper control you.

Every major spiritual battle is in the mind.
Charles Stanley

Big Idea for Parents

Count to t[...] angry with someone, don't say the first thing that comes to your mind. Instead, catch your breath and start counting until you are once again in control of your temper. If you count to a million and you're still counting, go to bed! You'll feel better in the morning.

Today's Prayer

Dear Lord, I can be so impatient,
and I can become so angry.
Calm me down, Lord, and make me
a patient, forgiving Christian,
today and every day of my life.
Amen

Words Are Important

Pleasant words are a honeycomb:
sweet to the taste and health to the body.
Proverbs 16:24 HCSB

Day 17

When we become angry, we may say things that are hurtful to other people. But when we strike out at others with the intention to hurt them, we are not doing God's will. God intends that His children treat others with patience, kindness, dignity, and respect. As Christians, we must do our best to obey our Creator.

Are you tempted to say an unkind word? Don't! Words are important, and once you say them, you can't call them back. But if you're wise, you won't need to!

Big Idea for Kids

Stop, think, then speak: If you want to make your words useful instead of hurtful, don't open your mouth until you've turned on your brain and given it time to warm up.

Words. Do you fully understand their power? Can any of us really grasp the mighty force behind the things we say? Do we stop and think before we speak, considering the potency of the words we utter?

Joni Eareckson Tada

Big Idea for Parents

Express yourself: Your children desperately need to hear that you love them . . . from you! If you're bashful, shy, or naturally uncommunicative, get over it.

Today's Prayer

Dear Lord, make me a person
of patience and kindness.
Make the things that I say
and do helpful to others,
so that through me,
they might see You.
Amen

Let's Be Patient With Parents

Honor your father and your mother.
Exodus 20:25 ICB

Day 18

Nobody's perfect, not even your parents. So the next time you're tempted to become angry with mom or dad for something they did or didn't do, stop and think about how much your parents do for you.

Sometimes, it's hard being a kid; that's for sure. But it can also be hard being a parent. Being a parent is a job with plenty of work to do, plenty of responsibilities to shoulder, and plenty of decisions to make. And if your parents make a bad decision every now and then, that's to be expected. So be patient with your parents . . . very patient. They've earned it.

Big Idea for Kids

Calm down . . . sooner rather than later! If you're angry with your mom or your dad, don't blurt out something unkind. If you can't say anything nice, go to your room and don't come out until you can.

> The child that never learns to obey
> his parents in the home will not obey
> God or man out of the home.
> Susanna Wesley

Big Idea for Parents

Hey Mom and Dad, how do you treat your parents? If you're lucky enough to have parents who are living, remember that the way you treat them is the way you're training your kids to treat you.

Today's Prayer

Dear Lord, make me patient and
respectful toward my parents;
let me give them honor and love;
and let my behavior be pleasing
to them . . . and to You.
Amen

Peace Is Wonderful

I leave you peace. My peace I give you.
I do not give it to you as the world does.
So don't let your hearts be troubled.
John 14:27 ICB

Day 19

Patience and peace go together. And the beautiful words from John 14:27 remind us that Jesus offers us peace, not as the world gives, but as He alone gives. We, as believers, can accept His peace or ignore it. When we accept the peace of Jesus Christ into our hearts, our lives are changed forever, and we become more loving, patient Christians.

Christ's peace is offered freely; it has already been paid for; it is ours for the asking. So let us ask . . . and then share.

Big Idea for Kids

Count to ten . . . but don't stop there!: If you're angry with someone, don't say the first thing that comes to your mind. Instead, catch your breath and start counting until you are once again in control of your temper.

Peace is better than a fortune.
St. Francis of Sales

Big Idea for Parents

Don't give fighting a fighting chance. When we grown-ups fight, our fights can have very grown-up consequences. If we are to be positive role models for our children, we must stand on principle, but we must also walk away from violence.

Today's Prayer

Dear Lord, help me to accept
Your peace and then to share it
with others, today and forever.
Amen

Avoiding Quarrels

It's a mark of good character to avert quarrels, but fools love to pick fights.

Proverbs 20:3 MSG

Day 20

In Proverbs King Solomon gave us wonderful advice for living wisely. Solomon warned that impatience and anger lead only to trouble. And he was right!

The next time you're tempted to say an unkind word or to start an argument, remember Solomon. He was one of the wisest men who ever lived, and he knew that it's always better to be patient. So remain calm, and remember that patience is best. After all, if it's good enough for a wise man like Solomon, it should be good enough for you, too.

Big Idea for Kids

Tempted to fight? Walk away. The best fights are those that never happen.

Argument is the worst sort of conversation.
Jonathan Swift

Big Idea for Parents

Be a booster, not a cynic: Even when our children make mistakes, we must not lose faith in them. Cynicism is contagious, and so is optimism. As parents, we must think and act accordingly.

Today's Prayer

Dear Lord, when I become angry,
help me to remember that You
offer me peace. Let me turn to You
for wisdom, for patience, and for
the peace that only You can give.
Amen

Always Growing Up

But grow in the special favor and knowledge
of our Lord and Savior Jesus Christ.
To him be all glory and honor, both now
and forevermore. Amen.

2 Peter 3:18 NLT

Day 21

When do we stop growing up? Hopefully never! If we keep studying God's Word, and if we obey His commandments, we will never be "fully grown" Christians. We will always be growing.

God intends that we continue growing in the love and knowledge of Christ. And when we do so, we become more patient, more loving, more understanding, and more Christ-like. And we keep growing and growing . . . and growing!

Big Idea for Kids

Read the Bible? Yes! Try to read the Bible with your parents every day. If they forget, remind them!

> The whole idea of belonging to Christ is
> to look less and less like we used to
> and more and more like Him.
> Angela Thomas

Big Idea for Parents

Don't be bothered by the minor inconveniences: life is far too short, and besides, your children are watching and learning . . . from you.

Today's Prayer

Dear Lord, let me keep learning about
Your love and Your Son as long as
I live. Make me a better person today
than I was yesterday, but not as good
a person as I can become tomorrow if
I continue to trust in You.

Amen

Let's Be Patient with Everybody!

I tell you the truth, anything you did
for even the least of my people here,
you also did for me.

Matthew 25:40 NCV

Day 22

The Bible tells us that we should be patient with everybody, not just with parents, teachers, and friends. In the eyes of God, all people are very important, so we should treat them that way.

Of course, it's easy to be nice to the people whom we want to impress, but what about everybody else? Jesus gave us clear instructions: He said that when we do a good deed for someone less fortunate than we are, we have also done a good deed for our Savior. And as Christians, that's exactly what we are supposed to do!

Big Idea for Kids

Everybody is a VIP: VIP means "Very Important Person." To God, everybody is a VIP, and we should treat every person with dignity, patience, and respect.

The times we find ourselves having to wait on others may be the perfect opportunities to train ourselves to wait on the Lord.

Joni Eareckson Tada

Big Idea for Parents

Remember that God's love doesn't simply flow to your children . . . it flows to you, too. And because God loves you, you can be certain that you, like your child, are wonderfully made and amazingly blessed.

Today's Prayer

Dear Lord, help me to be patient with everyone I meet. Help me to be respectful of all people, and help me to say kind words and do good deeds, today and every day.

Amen

Patience at Home

Foolish people lose their tempers,
but wise people control theirs.
Proverbs 29:11 NCV

Day 23

Sometimes, it's easiest to become angry with the people we love most. After all, we know that they'll still love us no matter how angry we become. But even though it's easy to become angry at home, it's usually wrong.

The next time you're tempted to become angry with a brother or a sister or a parent, remember that these are the people who love you more than anybody else! Then, calm down. Peace is always beautiful, especially when it's peace at your house.

Big Idea for Kids

Speak respectfully to everybody, starting with parents, grandparents, teachers, and other adults . . . but don't stop there. Be respectful of all people, including yourself!

The first essential for a happy home is love.
Billy Graham

Big Idea for Parents

Respectful behavior never goes out of style: Remember the good old days when children were supposed to be polite and respectful, especially to adults? For wise parents, those good old days are now.

Today's Prayer

Dear Lord, make me respectful of
all people, and when I become angry
with my family and friends,
let me be quick to forgive and forget.
Let me be a patient, kind, loving
Christian today and always.
Amen

Think First, Speak Later

The wise don't tell everything they know,
but the foolish talk too much and are ruined.
Proverbs 10:14 NCV

Day 24

When we become frustrated or tired, it's easier to speak first and think second. But that's not the best way to talk to people. The Bible tells us that "a good person's words will help many others." But if our words are to be helpful, we must put some thought into them.

The next time you're tempted to say something unkind, remember that your words can and should be helpful to others, not hurtful. God wants to use you to make this world a better place, and He will use the things that you say to help accomplish that goal . . . if you let Him.

Big Idea for Kids

When talking to other people, ask yourself this question: "How helpful can I be?"

The things we think are the things that feed our souls. If we think on pure and lovely things, we shall grow pure and lovely like them; and the converse is equally true.

Hannah Whitall Smith

Big Idea for Parents

Parents set the boundaries: Whether they realize it or not, parents (not kids) establish the general tone of the conversations that occur within their homes. And it's up to parents to ensure that the tone of those conversations is a tone that's pleasing to God.

Today's Prayer

Dear Lord, I want my words to help
other people. Let me choose my words
carefully so that when I speak,
the world is a better place because
of the things I have said.

Amen

If You Need Help, Ask God!

We pray that the Lord will lead your hearts into God's love and Christ's patience.

2 Thessalonians 3:5 ICB

Day 25

Do you need help in becoming a more patient person? If so, ask God; He's always ready, willing, and able to help. In fact, the Bible promises that when we sincerely seek God's help, He will give us the things we need.

So, if you want to become a better person, bow your head and start praying about it. And then rest assured that with God's help, you can change for the better . . . and you will!

Big Idea for Kids

Don't be too hard on yourself: you don't have to be perfect to be wonderful. God loves you . . . and you should, too.

Don't be afraid to ask your heavenly Father for anything you need. Indeed, nothing is too small for God's attention or too great for his power.

Dennis Swanberg

Big Idea for Parents

Parents should ask for help, too. If you need something, ask. And remember this: God is listening, and He wants to hear from you right now.

Today's Prayer

Dear Lord, I have so much to learn
and so many ways to improve myself,
but You love me just as I am.
Thank You for Your love and for
Your Son. And, help me to
become the person that You
want me to become.
Amen

What the Bible Says About It

Your word is like a lamp for my feet
and a light for my way.
Psalm 119:105 ICB

Day 26

Are you having trouble with your temper, or with anything else for that matter? The answer to your problems can be found in God's Holy Word: the Bible.

The Bible is God's instruction book for living. If you learn what the Bible says, and if you follow its instructions, you will be blessed now and forever. So get to know your Bible; it's never too soon to become an expert on God's Word.

Big Idea for Kids

Take care of your Bible! It's the most important book you own . . . by far!

> I believe the Bible is the best gift
> God has given to man.
>
> Abraham Lincoln

Big Idea for Parents

Daily devotionals never go out of style: are you too busy to lead a daily devotional with your family? If so, it's time to reorder your priorities.

Today's Prayer

Dear Lord, You have given me
a marvelous gift: the Holy Bible.
Let me read it and understand it
and believe it and follow
the commandments that I find there—
every day that I live.
Amen

A Little More Patient Every Day

Foolish people lose their tempers,
but wise people control theirs.
Proverbs 29:11 NCV

Do you want to become a person who is perfectly patient? And would you like to become that person today? Sorry! You've got to be patient, even when it comes to becoming more patient!

It's impossible to grow up all at once. Instead, we must grow up a little each day. And that's the way it is with patience: we can become a little more patient each day, and we should try our best to do so. When we do, we grow up to become wise adults. And just think: we will have acquired all that wisdom one day at a time!

Big Idea for Kids

Be patient with others and with yourself: an important part of growing up is learning to be patient with others and with yourself. And one more thing: learn from everybody's mistakes, especially your own.

> Every day we live is a priceless gift of God, loaded with possibilities to learn something new, to gain fresh insights.
>
> Dale Evans Rogers

Big Idea for Parents

Be patient with your child's impatience: children are supposed to be more impulsive than adults; after all, they're still kids. So be understanding of your child's limitations and understanding of his imperfections.

Today's Prayer

Dear Lord, let me become a little more
grown up every day. Let me become
the kind of person that You want
me to be, Lord, and then let me keep
growing up every day that I live.
Amen

When Things Go Wrong

Be patient when trouble comes.
Pray at all times.
Romans 12:12 ICB

From time to time, all of us have to face troubles and disappointments. When we do, God is always ready to protect us. Psalm 147 promises, "He heals the brokenhearted" (v. 3 NIV), but it doesn't say that He heals them instantly. Usually, it takes time for God to heal His children.

If you find yourself in any kind of trouble, pray about it and ask God for help. And then be patient. God will work things out, just as He has promised, but He will do it in His own time and according to His own plan.

Big Idea for Kids

You can make it right . . . if you think you can! If you've made a mistake, apologize. If you've broken something, fix it. If you've hurt someone's feelings, apologize. If you failed at something, try again. There is always something you can do to make things right.

Each problem is a God-appointed instructor.
Charles Swindoll

Big Idea for Parents

The best way to teach patience is to demonstrate it: Our actions speak so loudly that they usually drown out our words.

Today's Prayer

Dear Lord, sometimes life is so hard,
but with You, there is always hope.
Keep me mindful that there is nothing
that will happen today that You
and I can't handle together.

Amen

When You're in a Hurry

Wait patiently on the Lord.
Be brave and courageous.
Yes, wait patiently on the Lord.
Psalm 27:14 NLT

Sometimes, the hardest thing to do is to wait. This is especially true when we're in a hurry and when we want things to happen now, if not sooner! But God's plan does not always happen in the way that we would like or at the time of our own choosing. Still, God always knows best.

Sometimes, even though we may want something very badly, we must still be patient and wait for the right time to get it. And the right time, of course, is determined by God, not by us.

Big Idea for Kids

Controlling yourself by slowing yourself down: Sometimes, the best way to control yourself is to slow yourself down. Then, you can think about the things you're about to do before you do them.

Some of us would do more for the Lord if we did less.

Vance Havner

Big Idea for Parents

Make an Appointment with Your Child . . . and Keep It: If your find it difficult to find enough time for your child, put him or her on your daily calendar and then keep the appointment.

Today's Prayer

Dear Lord, I want to be able to control
myself better and better each day.
Help me find better ways to behave
myself in ways that are pleasing to You.
Amen

It Starts on the Inside

God's holy people must be patient.
They must obey God's commands
and keep their faith in Jesus.
Revelation 14:12 ICB

Day 30

Where does patience start? It starts on the inside and works its way out. When our hearts are right with God, patience is a natural consequence of our love for Him.

Psalm 37:7 commands us to wait patiently for God, but, for most of us, waiting quietly for Him is difficult. Why? Because we are imperfect people who seek immediate answers to our problems. We don't like to wait for anybody or anything. But, God instructs us to be patient in all things, and that is as it should be. After all, think how patient God has been with us.

Big Idea for Kids

God and your parents have been patient with you . . . now it's your turn to be patient with others.

Your thoughts are the determining factor
as to whose mold you are conformed to.
Control your thoughts and you control
the direction of your life.

Charles Stanley

Big Idea for Parents

Faith in God is contagious, and when it comes to your child's spiritual journey, no one's faith is more contagious than yours! Act, pray, praise, and trust God with the certain knowledge that your child is watching . . . carefully!

Today's Prayer

Dear Lord, give me patience in matters
both great and small. You have been
patient with me, Lord; let me be loving,
patient, and kind to my family
and to my friends, today and always.
Amen

With Love in Your Heart

So these three things continue forever:
faith, hope, and love.
And the greatest of these is love.
1 Corinthians 13:13 ICB

Day 31

The words of 1 Corinthians 13:13 remind us that love is God's commandment: "But now abide faith, hope, love, these three; but the greatest of these is love" (v. 13 NASB). Faith is important, of course. So is hope. But, love is more important still.

Christ loved us first, and, as Christians, we should return His love by sharing it. Today, let's share Christ's love with our families and friends. When we do, we'll discover that a loving heart is also a patient heart. And, we'll discover that the more we love, the more patient we become.

Big Idea for Kids

Pray for a heart that is loving and patient, and remember that God answers prayer!

In the presence of love, miracles happen.
Robert Schuller

Big Idea for Parents

Validate Your Children: In your own eyes, your children are perfect, or nearly so. Make certain that you communicate your love, your admiration, and your devotion many times each day.

Today's Prayer

Dear Lord, give me a heart that is filled with love, patience, and concern for others. Slow me down and calm me down so that I can see the needs of other people. And then, give me a loving heart so that I will do something about the needs that I see.

Amen

Bible Verses
to Remember

Be gentle to all, able to teach, patient.

2 Timothy 2:24 NKJV

Do for other people the same things you want them to do for you.

Matthew 7:12 ICB

Foolish people are always
getting into quarrels,
but avoiding quarrels
will bring you honor.

Proverbs 20:3 ICB

The right word spoken at
the right time is as beautiful as
gold apples in a silver bowl.

Proverbs 25:11 ICB

Patience is better than pride.

Ecclesiastes 7:8 NLT

Show respect for
all people.
Love the brothers and
sisters of God's family.

1 Peter 2:17 ICB

Be still before the Lord and wait patiently for Him.

Psalm 37:7 NIV

Do not worry about anything.
But pray and ask God
for everything you need.

Philippians 4:6 ICB

If you have two shirts,
share with the person
who does not have one.
If you have food,
share that too.

Luke 3:11 ICB

Be still, and know that I am God . . . .

Psalm 46:10 KJV

Let everyone see that
you are considerate
in all you do.

Philippians 4:5 NLT

Blessed are the peacemakers, because they will be called sons of God.

Matthew 5:9 HCSB

Always be humble and gentle. Be patient and accept each other with love.

Ephesians 4:2 ICB

Whatever you do, do everything for God's glory.

1 Corinthians 10:31 HCSB

I will give you a new heart
and put a new spirit
in you . . . .

Ezekiel 36:26 NIV

This is love for God:
to obey his commands.

1 John 5:3 NIV

Patience is better than strength.

Proverbs 16:32 ICB